# A NOTE TO PARENTS

When your children are ready to "step into reading," giving them the right books—and lots of them—is as crucial as giving them the right food to eat. **Step into Reading Books** present exciting stories and information reinforced with lively, colorful illustrations that make learning to read fun, satisfying, and worthwhile. They are priced so that acquiring an entire library of them is affordable. And they are beginning readers with an important difference—they're written on four levels.

**Step 1 Books,** with their very large type and extremely simple vocabulary, have been created for the very youngest readers. **Step 2 Books** are both longer and slightly more difficult. **Step 3 Books,** written to mid-second-grade reading levels, are for the child who has acquired even greater reading skills. **Step 4 Books** offer exciting nonfiction for the increasingly proficient reader.

Children develop at different ages. **Step into Reading Books,** with their four levels of reading, are designed to help children become good—and interested—readers *faster*. The grade levels assigned to the four steps—preschool through grade 1 for Step 1, grades 1 through 3 for Step 2, grades 2 and 3 for Step 3, and grades 2 through 4 for Step 4—are intended only as guides. Some children move through all four steps very rapidly; others climb the steps over a period of several years. These books will help your child "step into reading" in style!

*Library of Congress Cataloging-in-Publication Data*
Standiford, Natalie. The bravest dog ever: The true story of Balto (Step into reading. A Step 2 book) SUMMARY: Recounts
the life of Balto, the sled dog who saved Nome, Alaska, in 1925 from a diphtheria epidemic by delivering medicine through
a raging snowstorm. ISBN 0-394-89695-5 (pbk.) — 0-394-99695-X (lib. bdg.) 1. Balto (Dog)—Juvenile literature. 2. Sled
dogs—Alaska—Nome—Biography—Juvenile literature. 3. Diphtheria—Alaska—Nome—Prevention—Juvenile literature.
[1. Balto (Dog). 2. Sled dogs. 3. Dogs. 4. Diphtheria—Alaska—Nome. 5. Alaska—History] I. Cook, Donald, ill. II. Title.
III. Series. SF428.7.S7 1989 636.7'3 89-3465

Manufactured in the United States of America 30

STEP INTO READING is a trademark of Random House, Inc.

Step into Reading™

# The Bravest Dog Ever
## The True Story of
# BALTO

By Natalie Standiford
Illustrated by Donald Cook

A Step 2 Book

Random House 🏠 New York

This is a true story

about a very brave dog.

His name was Balto.

The year was 1925.

Balto lived in Nome, Alaska.

Nome was a frontier town.

Most of the year it was buried

under ice and snow.

In winter there was no way

to travel through all that ice and snow.

Not on planes or trains or boats or cars.

The only way to travel in Alaska

was by dog sled.

Balto was a sled dog.

He worked for a gold-mining company
not far from Nome.

He helped carry food and tools
to the miners.

It was a good life for a sled dog.

Balto's driver was named Gunnar.

Gunnar made Balto his lead dog.

The lead dog runs in front
of the team.

He follows the trail.

All the other dogs do
whatever the lead dog does.
So the lead dog has to be
the smartest and strongest dog of all.

One cold winter day

a terrible thing happened in Nome.

Two children got very sick.

Their parents called the doctor.

He was the only doctor

in the whole town.

When the doctor saw the children

he was very worried.

The children had a terrible sickness.

It was called diphtheria (dif-THEER-ee-ah).

The doctor did not have

the medicine he needed.

Without the medicine

the children would die.

Without the medicine

many other people in Nome

would get diphtheria and die too.

The doctor knew

he had to get some medicine—fast.

The hospital in Anchorage, Alaska,

had the medicine.

But Anchorage was 800 miles away.

The doctors in Anchorage

put the medicine on a train.

But soon the train got stuck

in the deep snow.

The train was still 700 miles

from Nome!

The people of Nome held a meeting.

Everyone was very scared.

"What are we going to do?"

asked the doctor.

"We have to get that medicine."

At last someone said,

"What about a dog-sled relay?

When one team of dogs gets tired,

a new team will be ready to take over."

The room buzzed with excitement.

That did seem like the quickest way

to get the medicine.

But the doctor frowned.

"It will still take about fifteen days.

That's a long time. Too long."

Maybe the doctor was right.

But there was no other choice.

So the mayor spoke over the radio.

"Please help!" he said.

"We need the best drivers and dogs

to help save our town!"

Gunnar heard the mayor on the radio.

Gunnar knew he had the best dog team

and the best lead dog.

Balto would come to the rescue.

ALASKA

NOME
SAFETY
BLUFF
GOLOVIN
SHAKTOOLIK
KOTUKUK
KALTAG
RUBY
TOLOVANA
NENANA
ANCHORAGE

On January 27, 1925,

the race to Nome began.

Twenty-one dog teams

were in the relay.

Each team waited at a different stop.

N
W · E
S

0    100    200    300
MILES

The first driver took the medicine
from the train.
He wrapped it in fur
to keep it from freezing.
Then he drove his dogs
as fast as he could to the second stop.
He made his run in good time.

But soon the wind began to blow hard.

The air grew colder.

A blizzard was coming!

It was one of the worst storms ever.

Still the race went on.

Somehow each dog team made it

to the next stop.

In one team, two dogs froze to death.

So the driver hitched himself

to the sled.

He helped the rest of his dogs

pull through the storm.

Gunnar and Balto waited

at their stop in Bluff.

They were going to run 31 miles

from Bluff to Point Safety.

That was the second-to-last part

of the race.

But the storm had slowed things down.

Gunnar had been waiting for two days.

He did not sleep.

He wanted to be ready to go

as soon as the medicine arrived.

At last Gunnar heard dogs barking.

The medicine was here!

He put it on the sled

with a small stove and a little food.

Then he hitched up his dogs.

Balto stood proudly in the lead.

Gunnar cracked his whip.

"Mush!" he cried.

That meant "go."

The team ran out into the snowy night.

At first the team made good time.

But soon snowdrifts blocked the trail.

The dogs sank up to their necks

in snow.

They could not move.

Some began to panic.

But not Balto.

He stayed calm.

That helped the other dogs

while Gunnar dug them out

of the snow.

At last the team was on its way again.

Then the team crossed a frozen river.

The dogs and the sled

slipped and skidded on the ice.

Oh, no! Over went the sled.

Gunnar got it up again.

But the medicine was gone!

Wildly Gunnar dug for the medicine.

He could not see

through the heavy snow.

But at last he felt the package.

He put it back on the sled.

The team kept going

across the river.

Suddenly Balto stopped short.

"Mush, Balto!" shouted Gunnar.

But Balto did not move.

Then Gunnar saw why.

The ice was cracking!

If the team fell into the river,

they would all drown.

Balto had stopped just in time.

"Smart dog!" Gunnar told him.

Then he saw that Balto's feet were wet.

If they froze,

Balto would never walk again.

Quickly Gunnar unhitched Balto

from the sled.

He led the dog

to a patch of powdery snow.

Gunnar rubbed Balto's paws

in the powder.

Soon they were dry.

Balto was ready to go once more.

Balto led the team

around the cracking ice.

At last they reached

solid land again.

Were they still on the trail?

Gunnar had no idea.

The snow blew so hard,

Gunnar could not see

his own hands.

But Balto had run this trail
many times before.
Now it was all up to him.

Finally the storm died down.

Gunnar saw Point Safety just ahead.

"Balto did it!" thought Gunnar.

He couldn't wait to warm his hands

by a cozy fire.

But all the lights were out

at Point Safety.

Was the next driver there?

Gunnar did not know.

And there was no time to find out.

So Gunnar and Balto did not stop.

They had never been so tired.

But they raced on through the night

toward Nome.

It was just before dawn.

The sky began to glow.

In the town of Nome

everyone was sleeping.

Gunnar and his team pulled into town.

They had made it!

Balto was too tired to bark.

They had been on the trail

for 20 hours straight.

They had driven 53 miles!

Gunnar took the medicine to the doctor.

The doctor was surprised.

He thought it would take 15 days

to get the medicine.

But Gunnar delivered it

after only five and a half days!

"Thank you, Gunnar!" said the doctor.

"You are a hero!"

"Balto is the hero," said Gunnar.

"I could not have done it without him."

The doctor went right to work.

He gave the medicine

to all the sick people.

In a few days they would be well.

The town of Nome was saved.

DAILY PAPER

NOME SAVED!

SLED DOG BRAVES
BLIZZARD, DELIVERS
DIPHTHERIA MEDICINE!

NOME, ALASKA

All over America

people cheered for Balto.

They read about his bravery

in the newspaper.

Balto was the most famous dog

in the world.

A year later

the people of New York City

put up a statue of Balto.

It still stands in Central Park.

Lots of children play on the statue.

They remember Balto,

the bravest dog ever!

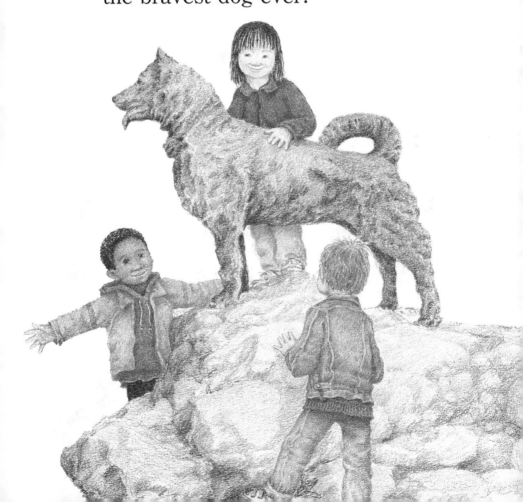